Don't Cry Out Loud!

Sandra Mullings Levingston

©2018 Sandra Mullings Levingston
ISBN-13:
978-1707907625

Oklahoma

This book is dedicated to my mother, Mrs. Katherine Mullings.

Don't Cry Out Loud!

Sandra Mullings Levingston

Chapter 1

The House That Mama Loved

By the time the firemen arrived, it was too late to do much of anything, except try to keep the fire under control and isolated to prevent it from spreading elsewhere. I do not know who called the fire department. It must have been one of the neighbors or some concerned passerby. For sure, it was not me because we did not even have a phone. Somehow Uncle Jerry had found out because he was there answering all those usual questions for the investigative report that is done when a place burns down.

Mama had gone with Aunt Bonnie, Uncle Jerry's wife, to Tulsa that day on one of their shopping trips. She kept me home from school to watch after the two little boys. No one had to twist my arm to keep me home. I did not like going to school there in Broken Arrow. Some time had passed, so we were not exactly new students anymore, but I still had not made any real friends except for one girl who lived near us. We did not have any classes together, and once we got off the bus in the morning, didn't see each other again unless we passed each other in the hallway.

I wanted to see those kids who had been my lifelong friends; to stand in one spot and turn in a slow circle to see mountains in every direction; to see orchards hanging heavy with pears, plums and walnuts; to be awakened in the middle of the night by the wonderful smell of that coffee Mama fixed for Daddy when he would be called out to light the smudge pots; to hear the sound of the wind machines kicking in, blowing through the orchards to protect them from moisture in frost; to be called to lunch by the noon whistle that sounded every day; to look out at recess time and see Grandma Burnett on top of the roof hammering away; to hear the honk of the Sunday School van and pull the ropes that rang our church bell; to sit on the pew next to someone who's always known me and sing hymns of praise to lift my spirit.

But Mama loved this house in Broken Arrow. Except for the inconvenience of no indoor bathroom, it was the nicest place in which she had ever lived. It was located just a couple of miles out of town, but rural enough to allow us some privacy and room for us kids to play. Daddy had a nice Garden space and we even had a couple of milk cows there. There was sufficient room for us all to sleep in a fair amount of comfort. The place has been well kept, and it was a home of which Mama could be proud for a change. I figured with her liking that place so much, we would be staying there for a long, long time.

That morning dreaded thoughts of living out the rest of my life in Oklahoma kept pressing my mind. I just could not bear the idea of having to stay there, and somehow, I just was not going to any longer. There was nothing holding me there, no one could stop me from leaving. So, after making a bunch of sandwiches and rounding up the boys, we set out walking. We thought we had walked at least a mile or so. The ground was still partially covered from the last snow. It was chilly outside, and the boys little hands and faces were red from exposure to the cold. What was I thinking? Had my sanity left me? We were two thousand miles away from our old California home. There we were barely a mile of the distance and already tired and half frozen to death. There was no choice but to turn back before we all caught pneumonia.

Now the firemen were everywhere. We stood out of their way near the road. I held tight to the boys' hands to keep them from running toward the flaming house. I felt sad to watch all of our possessions burning to cinders, and felt scared that someone would blame me. But I felt happy because that house was no longer an obstacle in our way of going back to our real home.

So many different emotions were making my mind numb. Standing there trembling with uncontrollable tears, my young eyes witnessed those powerful flames consume the house that Mama loved so well. At that moment my mind became a blur as it drifted from the present and slipped back to yesteryears.

Chapter 2
They Say

They say Daddy used to push Mama in a swing lots of times when he was twelve and she was only six years old. Mama and Daddy had grown up in Johnston County, Oklahoma, with their families and close friends. Grandpa Randy had lost his hand, so Daddy had to quit school after third grade to help support his family. Daddy had lived most all his life in Oklahoma, until he entered service, but had been able to help buy a farm for his folks and planned to come back to it upon discharge. For some reason, his folks sold the place and moved to

Arizona, while Daddy was still in the Navy.

Mama's folks had left Oklahoma, too, a couple of years earlier, and ended up in Kelseyville, California. Grandpa and Grandma Smith divorced when Mama was only ten years old and Grandpa took custody of both her and Uncle Leroy. The two older girls had already married and left home. Soon after the divorce, Grandpa moved Mama and Uncle Leroy to Denison, Texas, and that's where she got back in contact with Daddy.

He was still in the service, lonely and homesick. Daddy's folks had written Mama with his address and ask her to write him, so they became pen pals. It had been four years since they had seen one another and there was a lot to catch up on. The closeness they'd felt as children was rekindled, and through all those letters they realized their deep love for each other. Soon after Daddy was discharged, he and Mama got married in Denison on July 19, 1947.

Mama was a daddy's girl, but must have missed Grandma really terribly to leave Grandpa there in Denison and move back to California soon after she and Daddy married. They say Grandpa had spoiled her, and Mama expected much of the same treatment from Daddy. She took his first paycheck and spent it all on new clothing for herself. She was just a confused little girl of fourteen, who was used to getting what she wanted, but I am sure she tried her best to be a good wife, too.

No one had ever taught Mama the skills necessary to be a homemaker. She could not cook nor sew. The first time she ever baked turned out so disastrous that she dug a hole and buried it in the backyard, to keep Daddy from finding out. Daddy must have had to help his mother while growing up, because he was able to sort of fill in the gaps that were missing in Mama's upbringing. They say he helped Grandma Renie make all the clothes for Mama and Daddy's first baby.

Wesley was born to them before Mama and Daddy's first anniversary. He was sick from the start with childhood leukemia. He could not drink anything except goat's milk, and not much of that stayed with him. He was not gaining any weight. They knew Wesley would not be with them long, so Daddy planned a trip to Arizona in order for his folks to see the baby. Wesley died soon after they arrived in El Mirage. What torment she must have experienced as lifeless little Wesley had to be pried from Mama's trembling young arms.

My parents stayed in Arizona for a while. It was hard to think about leaving Wesley out there in that cemetery, and Mama was pregnant again, so they did not want to take any chances. Verna was born on October 1, 1949. She had big blue eyes and platinum curls, a picture of health and a very happy child. It helped ease the loss and grief they felt to have such a precious little baby girl.

Verna was an infant when my parents moved to Alturas, a small Northern California town near the Oregon border. Daddy convinced the railroad company to hire him by offering to work for free until he was fully trained and had proven himself to be a valuable worker. Life must have been pretty good for them in Alturas because Mama and Daddy stayed there for five years. Four more children were born to them there, I being the third of those four. It was a wonder my health at birth was as good as it was because Mama was in a car wreck during her eight month of pregnancy with me. She and Daddy had driven to Klamath Falls, as usual to buy groceries. It was early September and there should not have been any traveling problems, but it was cold and over the mountains the car hit a slick spot and spun out of control. Mama was thrown out of the car face forward and slid on her stomach for quite a distance. That trauma put her into labor a month early, but I was born, screaming and healthy, and Mama was fine except for a few broken ribs and a lot of bruises.

Mama had complications a year later too, with her next pregnancy, and Linda was born six weeks early. She only weighed four pounds, five ounces, and was only sixteen inches Long. I was too young to remember, but they say she was an odd-looking little thing without any toenails, fingernails, eyebrows or lashes at first, and with lots of long black hair. Being premature resulted in Linda having underdeveloped lungs and serious bronchial problems. The climate in Alturas was far too cold for her to survive.

Mama and Daddy knew well the terrible pain of losing a baby and could not bear the thought of experiencing such heartache again, so they left the cool, mountain climate of Alturas and moved from one small California town to the next before deciding to move back to Arizona.

The climate of Arizona should have helped Linda more than it did. Things were still touch-and-go, and many times they were sure that they would lose her. The medical bills were mounting up. Daddy could not find a decent-paying job there either, so he and Mama decided to move the family to Tishomingo, Oklahoma, where Grandpa Smith then lived.

The doctors warned against such a move, claiming the humidity of Oklahoma would kill Linda, but she was not doing any good in Arizona, and Daddy had a wife and four other children to think about. He had to find a job that would better support them, or they were all going to starve to death. They say He told the doctors the cost of living was cheaper in Oklahoma, and the funeral expenses would be less expensive there too. I guess he knew that firsthand as well as anybody.

To everyone's amazement, Linda's lungs grew stronger in Oklahoma, and eventually the threat of losing her no longer existed. We probably would have stayed in Tishomingo but Grandma Renie, who still lived in Kelseyville California, was diagnosed with colon cancer. Mama needed to be near her.

Chapter 3

Hollyhocks Everywhere

Grandma Burnett had fiery, red hair that was sort of pushed out in an Afro Style. She always wore bright red lipstick which matched her hair. She had a round, smiling face, kind eyes, and laughed loud and jolly. She was short and stout, always wore overalls, and carried a hammer around everywhere she went to fix this or that.

Grandma Burnett was not really our grandmother, but everyone knew her as such. She and her husband built a group of brick red, wooden cabins on the hillside to the east of the highway, as

you are going north out of Kelseyville.
Her husband had died years before, but
rent from these cabins was Grandma
Burnett's livelihood, and she kept the
place going by herself.

My earliest memories are fond ones
of life at Burnett's cabins. That is
where Mama and Daddy moved us when we
left Tishomingo. And where I met both
of the little girls who became my
closest friends. We were all
preschoolers at the time. There are
hollyhocks everywhere, taller than any
of us kids, and we had fun playing
amongst them. We spent lots of time at

each other's houses because our mothers had become friends too.

We moved from the cabin so that Mama could be closer to and take better care of Grandma Renie. She lived in some apartments known to the town as "Cockroach Ally", and we moved there a few doors down from her. Grandma Renie had a dog named Shorty. We used to play with that old dog all the time, so he knew all of us kids well. One evening Mama sent me over to Grandma's to get something for her. I first knocked on the door and as usual, just started on into the front room, when Shorty attacked me. He jumped up on me, scratching my face. I never understood why he turned on me like that and it took me a long time to trust Shorty or any other dog again.

Floyd was a special person in our lives back then. He was Grandma Renie's second and last husband. He was a big, clumsy guy, illiterate and slow minded. He spoke with a speech impediment and lots of the townspeople made fun of him, but Floyd had a good heart. He loved us kids and we loved him. He, not realizing his own strength, and as an affectionate display, would grab hold of our ears and pull them half off when we came around. Floyd spent days scavenging around the town dump, searching for junk to sell. He always brought us discarded one-armed or one-legged baby dolls and trucks with the wheel or two missing, but we loved those broken toys and still got plenty of use from them. Grandma died on Valentine's Day in 1959, but Floyd remained a big part of our lives even after her death.

That year all of the kids were in school, except for Linda and me and of course the new baby, Terri. I would have gone to kindergarten there, but my right arm was in a cast all summer and the doctor would not release me to start school that fall. We girls had a bed with iron railings which set right below the window of our room. It was a warm day, so Mama had that window open to catch what little breeze was blowing. We knew better than to do so, but Linda was having a great time jumping on the bed while I was flipping myself over the rails. I flipped myself right out of that window and my arm hit hard against our butane tank nozzle.

Linda ran to get Mama, who hurried outside took one look at my mangled arm, and started to cry uncontrollably. For some reason my arm did not hurt as badly as it appeared to, so I told Mama it was okay and asked her not to cry. She was

pregnant with her eighth child, but Mama
still picked me up, carried me to the
car and rushed me to the doctor's office
where my arm was set and cast.

The doctor said I was fortunate
because if there had been slightly more
breakage, he would have been forced to
amputate my arm at the elbow.

Because of my broken arm I had to
spend most of all summer indoors. It was
boring and seemed unfair that the other
kids got to play outside. Mama felt
sorry for me and did let me go out once
to play on the bank of the little stream
that ran behind the apartments. Propped
up against a tree there was an old coil

bedspring someone had discarded. I was playing under them having a great time when one of the ornery little neighborhood boys knocked them over on top of me, delaying my cast removal for an entire two weeks. That ended my outdoor activities for the rest of the summer.

Finally, that wonderful day came when the cast was to come off. I was so happy at the idea of losing the cast until the doctor picked up his saw. I screamed thinking he had decided to go ahead and amputate my arm after all. Mama assured me the saw was only to split the cast so it would be removed. She said everything would be all right and of course it was.

That summer Linda and I played together all day long while all the older kids were in school. It was on such a day while we were making mud pies that we heard the strangest sound. She always was a "fraidy cat" and wanted to go inside, but I convinced Linda that all we heard was a dog barking.

Again, the weird noise sounded, and we looked up to see this strange looking, skinny animal with long, white hair and horns headed right for us. We had never seen such an animal before. One thing was for sure, this was no ordinary dog, and the sound it made was unlike any bark we had ever heard. We made a mad dash up the steps to the house to tell Mama what we had seen. After investigating, she lovingly laughed at us for being so scared and informed us this thing was just a goat.

Chapter 4

Trading Time

We set up chairs in the front yard and placed bed sheet curtains up across the front porch to pretend it was a stage. A minimal fee was charged, and then the performance began. Sometimes we would hula dance, and on other occasions we would have a skit to act out. Our audience was always pleased regardless of how we chose to entertain them.

Aunt Vie, Mama's sister, and her husband, Uncle Clyde, attended many of our shows. Aunt Vie had nicknames for all of us like "Little Bit" and "Kitten." She made the best walnut cake and would bring it for us. Uncle Clyde was tall, and his slenderness made him appear even taller. He was one of the happiest people we knew and laughed all the time. We kids pulled a lot of pranks on him. More than once we doctored his coffee with salt instead of the usual three teaspoons of sugar.

Uncle Clyde had a gypsy background and was mysterious about some things. He practiced some kind of magic that removed warts. He had gotten rid of one that was blocking Linda's vision when she was a baby and another off her right hand when she was a little older. He did not use any balms, but just said to believe it would disappear, and sure enough in a day or two the wart would be gone. He never told his secret and we asked him about it many times. I always believed his power was prayer.

We loved to see company such as Aunt Vie and Uncle Clyde. As the years went by Mama had learned to be an excellent cook and on special occasions, she did invite family over and fix her famous green chili burritos. They were made precisely like we all like them, so hot that the first bite gave us hiccups. Tears would run down Uncle Clyde's face when he ate those spicy burritos. We drank milk to cool our burning mouths, and Mama had to buy two gallons to have enough to go around for that one meal of green chili burritos.

At that time, we were living in a big house across from Parker's Market in Kelseyville. Bobby was born there. He was Mama and Daddy's ninth child. To me he was a real-life baby doll. I was only seven, but packed him around all of the time.

Leslie, our oldest living brother, tied the rope over a tree branch in the front yard of that house, and those brave enough climbed on top of Daddy's pickup and swung from it. The grocer's son, Logan, not to be outdone by Leslie, climbed up, placed the rope in his mouth and then thrust himself forward off that old pickup. All of his weight pulled on Logan's gums and he ended up in the dentist chair with a full mouth of busted, bleeding teeth.

We celebrated Halloween while living in that big house. It seems funny but I do not remember us ever spending Halloween anywhere besides Lake County, California. Most often we'd be home during Walnut season, which started right after the first of November. Our town had the strangest tradition. On the evening before Halloween we had to bring all the clothes pins in off the line, or they would be stolen. We never knew the origin of that strange custom nor what significance it had to the holiday.

We could hardly wait for Halloween to come. The school allowed us to come to class in full costume, and we got to parade around downtown. The hours between school and sundown though seemed unusually long. Finally, it would be dusk and time to go trick-or-treating. We would each start out with one grocery bag, fill it up, and then take it home to exchange for an empty one. By then the little kids would be tired, so they stayed home, and then some real fun began.

We did not have to walk slow any longer and hold on to little hands that were sticky from lollipops. The rest of us older kids still had to stay together, but we could run from house to house and cover a lot of ground before we had to be home. We had long discarded those hard-plastic masks, because dress-up no longer mattered. We were now in it for the loot. We seldom ever got candy at home, and that made Halloween an even more special time.

About the worst trick we pulled was to write on a few business establishments' windows with a bar of soap, but we knew there were more ornery things happening. Sometimes during Halloween night, the bell tower would be climbed, and someone would string the church bell across Finley's Bridge. We were never involved in that and never positively knew who the pranksters were, but we had our suspicions.

We had been everywhere else, and the highlight of our evening was going to the home of "Peepa Weepa." We called her that because it's what she would seem to be saying as we walked by her house. Her hair was cut short, and she dressed in men's clothing. She was thin and took long strides with those skinny legs when she walked, and she walked everywhere.

She never spoke to any of us, nor we her, so we never learned her real name or much of anything about her. But we sure knew where Peepa Weepa lived. Although none of us were brave enough to knock on her door, going past her house on Halloween was our ultimate test of bravery.

Our grocery bags would be full, and we would have to hurry home to make it back by our 9 o'clock curfew. Back then there did not seem to be any concern that the candy and other goodies were contaminated with dope, glass or razor blades. When we'd eaten our share, it was trading time. We would dump our loot on the floor and the deals commenced. Halloween evening was full of fun and excitement, and when our tired heads finally hit the pillow, we had no problem sleeping.

We got plenty of exercise walking those small-town streets of Kelseyville. The elementary school was located all the way across town from us, so we younger kids had a pretty good distance to travel every weekday. We usually enjoyed the walk, but in the rainy season it was not much fun. We had galoshes and raincoats but somehow would still be soaking wet by the time we got to school. Verna lucked out because we lived just down the hill from the high school. She even got to bring her friends home for lunch.

We also made lots of trips to the grocery store for Mama. She would write out a list that we handed to the clerk, who did the actual shopping for us. I remember walking home from Spalding's grocery and the big trucks would zoom by on their way to the highway. If there happened to be milk in my bag for extra leverage it would be all right, but if there was only bread the wind from the passing trucks caused me to be off balanced and fall right on my rump.

Many times, you would find us heading up to the high school with pint jars in a bowl in which to gather walnuts. Once there we would find us a rock hard enough to crack the nuts and a comfortable spot to sit on the ground. After hours of tediously cracking and picking out those black walnuts, we started back for home with our jars filled to the rim to claim a reward from Mama of a nickel or dime.

Life was simple and good in the little Northern California town of Kelseyville. We never watched much daytime television, so our minds were filled with imagination, and we had great times back then. We were far from rich, but we had each other and knew everybody. We had good friends there. Kelseyville was our home.

Chapter 5
Leaving Our Hearts Behind

We came home from school one day to find the car half packed. Where were we going? No one had mentioned a word about us going anywhere. Now Mama and Daddy were telling us that we were taking a trip to Arizona. We had no phone to call anyone to say goodbye. There was no time to tell our friends or teachers. Tomorrow we would just not be at school. After a few days everyone would wonder what happened to us. My heart sank. I was already home sick, and we had not even left yet.

Before dark we were headed out for I-5 South leaving our hearts behind with whatever other possessions we could not squeeze in or on top of the station wagon. It was so hard to leave like we did, but still the trip itself did spark some excitement. Mama would start singing some old familiar tune, we kids would join in, and before you knew it, we were halfway down the state and had gone through every song that we could all call to mind. All of that singing seemed to be our way to help ease the pain of leaving home and lessen the fear of the unknown that lay ahead of us.

One thing is for sure those were rare times of total family togetherness. There were eight of us kids at that time

and some of us weren't so small anymore.
The older kids took turns riding up
front with Daddy and Mama, and sometimes
Mama held Bobby in her lap to. The
backseat had been let down and packed
boxes placed on the floorboard to make
an even surface for the rest of us kids
to ride.

We had sardines-packed kids,
blankets, and pillows everywhere. But
for a little while there was no ton of
dirty dishes to do, no floors to sweep
and mop, no bathtubs or commode to scrub
down, and no mountains of laundry to
wash, hang out, fold, and iron.

Daddy would not stop often and sometimes it would be a good distance between the market where we bought our food and the rest area where we finally got to eat. The longer the wait, the better our bologna sandwiches and bananas tasted. Mama usually brought us cream cookies, and the milk we drank caused them to melt in our mouths. With our bellies full, legs stretched a little, we would pile back in the car and head out again. There would be no more stops for hours unless the car needed gas. Daddy hated to stop for gas too. He seemed to think he could squeeze in a few more miles on fumes from an empty tank, and more than once we would run out of gas. He ended up hitchhiking to the nearest station with a gas can in his hand.

All too soon that dreaded Tehachapi Mountain lay before us. There is a nice four-lane highway across it now, but back then the pass was in terrible need of repair. The road was caving in on the cliff side, and fog so thick that at times Daddy put Mama behind the wheel as he walked ahead of the car with a flashlight so we could make it across. Someone had gone over the edge. We could see the rescue teams trying to assist them. Scared for our lives, we kids were screaming and crying, which did not help Mama a bit from being so nervous. She yelled at us to keep quiet so that she could concentrate, and we all prayed for our guardian angels' protection. Finally, we made it to the top of the mountain where the little town of Tehachapi sits. We got to stop there and get out of the car for a few minutes, catch our breaths and finally feel the joy of survival.

The desert awaited us as we drove down the mountain. It seemed about a hundred miles to Barstow, which was the next town. That long stretch was dotted here and there with Whiting Brothers service stations, but other than that it was barren. It was so hot, and we had no air conditioner. Daddy timed most of our desert travel for the evening. It was so amazing to me how cool the nights were in a place so blazing hot during daytime hours. I remember coming across a sign that someone had placed out in the middle of the Mojave that read "Hottest place this side of hell." We kids were always astonished at how big the desert moon appeared to be.

The next morning that huge, gorgeous sun came up over the horizon to welcome us to Arizona. Daybreak revealed interesting cacti and rolling tumbleweeds. From time to time we would see fascinating mini whirlwinds. We reached Grandma Mullings house in El Mirage before the morning was over.

Chapter 6

I Want To Go Home

Grandma Mullings stood only about four foot ten, if even that, was stocky built, and a little on the plump side. She was a strict person but treated us kids kindly enough, and it was nice to be around her for a change. All of Daddy's folks lived in Arizona, and we barely knew them.

Grandma had extra mattresses stacked on every bed and would pull them off at night, to make sure all of us had a comfortable place to sleep. She would fix a huge breakfast and a big mid-afternoon dinner. Seemed strange to us to only eat twice a day. We found a way of sneaking in an in between snack though.

Grandma had a pomegranate tree in her yard. We would find a stick or something long enough to knock loose a couple of those pomegranates. We loved their bittersweet taste and they'd tide us over until mealtime.

George was a border in Grandma's house. He lived with her for years. Grandpa Randy had died long ago, but George was like a grandpa to us. He made us a swing on the tree out in the front yard and would push us real high in it.

He liked being around kids and was good to us.

We were in Arizona for an awful reason this time. Our cousin, Benny, had been killed. He was using a chainsaw on top of a pickup when the saw hit a knot in the tree. The saw bounced back on him, cutting Benny through the neck and chest. After falling from the truck there was evidence that he had gotten up somehow and ran a few feet, then collapsed and died. What a tragic death for anybody, but especially tragic for a kid of only sixteen years.

We were only supposed to be there to attend the funeral. We had left almost everything behind and had not even pulled a trailer with us. We had no furniture, dishes, nothing with which to set up housekeeping. I could not believe that Mama and Daddy had decided to stay in Arizona.

Oh, how I dreaded that first day of the new school. We had to enroll ourselves. Mama could not come along because she had three little ones still at home, and Daddy had driven the car to work. She sent a note along with us to the school with all of the pertinent information, but still the office worker hassled us about transfer papers, which we did not have because we had not even withdrawn from our school back home. The secretary gave us a hard time.

The teacher took me in front of the class and introduced me as a new student. All of the kids stared at me. I never felt so alone. Leslie had failed first grade, so he and I were both in third then, but they would not place us in the same classroom. Everyone thought we were twins and that was pretty neat to me, but Leslie did not like it one bit.

Leslie was always protective of me in our younger years. We were supposed to be eligible for free lunches, but no one had informed the cafeteria cashier, and she made me go all the way back to the end of the lunch line so that she could take care of her other "non-problem" kids and have time to deal with me. Knowing the class bell would ring before I had time to go through that long line again, I just wandered around on the playground alone, hungry, crying, and wondering what I had done so wrong to be sent to the end of the line. Back home the teachers on cafeteria duty would sometimes do that to a kid if they had taken cuts or misbehaved in some way. This was only my first day at school in El Mirage and I had already been scolded twice.

I never got in trouble at school back home, well except for that one time in first grade. The teacher had told us those who did not have their papers completed by the time the bell rang would have to stay in at recess time to get it done. I did not get done, but decided to go out anyway. All during recess, I kept thinking about what would happen to me when we went back inside. Sure enough, the teacher had collected our papers and two of us girls had not obeyed her. She gave us both a lecture and a paddling. That left me embarrassed enough and with such an impression that I never deliberately disobeyed the teacher again.

I hated this new school. School was fun back home. We always got to do interesting things. One day the teacher showed us how to make yeast rolls. We kids were all so proud of how well they turned out. I can still remember how wonderful they smelled and how delicious they tasted. No one ever made me go hungry at home. That is what I was thinking about when Leslie found me on the playground. He had once again come to my rescue and straightened everything out with the cashier. Leslie made sure I got lunch that day, but we could not stop the bell from ringing. So, there I was the new kid coming in late to class and in trouble again.

Glenn was born while we were in El Mirage. Daddy could not afford a hospital bill, so he was delivered right in the doctor's office. Now there were nine of us kids, and Daddy still had not found a decent job locally. He decided to go find work in Safford. It was too far away to commute. We stayed in that little house they had rented in El Mirage while Daddy went on to Safford to find a job and a place for us to live. Money was really tight, and we did not have a lot of food to eat, but we never went hungry. I do remember eating a lot of grilled cheese sandwiches. Mama got the cheese from the commodity program.

When school was out Daddy came back for us. We all hated it there in Safford. We didn't have any furniture on which to sit and only a mattress on the floor where we slept. Those desert days were hot. The water tasted like sulfur. We were miserable. Mama had us gang up on Daddy and sing, "I Want To Go Home" and it sort of worked. He packed us up, but we weren't going home, we were Oklahoma bound. Tishomingo was

a day and night's travel away.

Chapter 7

Somewhere Besides Home

If we had to be somewhere besides home Tishomingo was the place to be. Most everyone there was related to us either on Grandpa Smith's or Grandma Renie's side. Those who were not relatives were lifelong friends and friendly people. Grandpa Smith had moved back to Tish with his third wife and two children.

It did not seem appropriate to call his kids aunt and uncle because they were just about my age. Grandpa liked to eat bread that he dipped in coffee, which was poured out into a saucer. He liked snow cones too, and we would frequently walk down with him to get one. He sure seemed tall to us, and for an elderly person Grandpa could certainly walk fast. He lived in a little broken-down shack. We used to have fun gathering and eating the wild garlic that grew out behind it.

We had threats of severe storms almost daily that spring. Grandpa was not afraid of much of anything, especially tornadoes. Even when a twister was sighted, he would not seek shelter, but sit rocking in an old chair on his rickety porch watching the storm pass by. You would not find Aunt Minnie and Aunt Altie anywhere but the storm shelter upon the first boom of thunder. They were Grandma Renie's sisters, the cutest little old ladies I'd ever seen. Aunt Altie was taller and thin, and Aunt Minnie was short and round. They would walk all the way across town to visit us. They both dipped snuff, and when we saw them walking up, we would run to find them a spit can. They lived right across the street from one another. Aunt Altie was a widow who lived with two of her bachelor sons. Aunt Minnie's husband plowed garden plots with a mule team. You could see old Alvin all of the time with his team driving the wagon down the road to some job he had contracted to do.

Uncle Jonie, Grandma Renie's brother, lived there in Tish too. He and his wife had a whole house full of kids. They were the only family we ever knew who had more kids than us. Uncle Dugan was another one of Grandma's brothers. He was short and round also. He did not live in Tish but used to come visit us once in a while. He was always good to us and brought us bags of candy when he came. Mama told us he was a kleptomaniac, and said that he had even stolen a car off of a showroom floor. He had been to prison. It was hard to imagine him as an ex-convict. We thought only bad people went to prison, and for sure Uncle Dugan was no bad guy.

Our ever-beloved Aunt Ruth lived in Tish also. She was not related to us but we're still family, nevertheless. She knew Daddy and Mama when they were children. Ruth lived in little house with her husband and four kids. She was soft-spoken and used slang that would tickle us. We poked fun at the Okie accent of her kids, and they poked fun of ours. Daddy always tried to bring Ruth a gunny sack of English walnuts, which seemed like nothing to us having been raised around them, but they were a real luxury in that part of Oklahoma. Ruth would cry both when we came and when we left.

We kids all got the chickenpox that summer. Just about the time one of us seemed to be recovering, another would get sick. What a mess! Mama had to keep hopping to nurse all of us back to health.

That summer sure passed fast. It seemed like we had no sooner got to Oklahoma then we were packing up and heading back for California. It was nearly August, and pear season would be starting back home. Going home sounded great to us kids, but leaving Grandpa and other Oklahoma relatives and friends was hard. Getting back home was not going to be any fun either. The misery of a cross-country trip with nine kids who had to ride with arms and legs atop each other, covered with blankets that had been peed and puked on, with no money available to rent a room and rest and bathe, is something that you would just have to experience to understand the great degree of misery involved.

Chapter 8

In The Boonies

If you follow Kelsey Creek Road out of town about six miles on past that winding canyon road about a half a mile or so, you will come up on two little houses sitting together on the left side of the road. Just a little ways after those places there is an old dirt road to the left that used to lead to a rickety bridge that crossed the creek. You will somehow have to get across the creek and go about another mile before you were officially arrived at the boonies. That is where we lived when we returned from Oklahoma.

Our place was at the foot of Mount Konocti. The other kids took hikes up the mountain and I got brave enough once to try it, but could only make it part of the way. Leslie came to piggyback me down. Just about the time he started to take a step, we heard that familiar rattle and looked down to see a coil Diamondhead Rattler ready to strike. Leslie knew enough not to move, and froze in his steps screaming to Mama for help. She came running to our rescue and did not hesitate one moment to worry about endangering herself. She did not stop to wonder whether or not she could run halfway up the mountainside either.

She just grabbed the hoe and headed toward us. With one swift whack, Mama chopped that snake's head off and carried the thing home putting it in a jar to show Daddy when he got home from work.

One day while we girls were cleaning the house, Linda ran and saying, "Mama, there's a huge cat outside and it is staring right at me!" Mama looked out of the kitchen window. She did not see anything and figured this was just another figment of Linda's wild imagination. But Linda was so insistent that Mama decided to go outside and take a closer look. She spotted the cat sitting in the shadows of a nearby tree. Mama rounded up the rest of the little kids and brought them into the house. She filled a pan with water and she and Leslie went back out. Leslie held the barbed wire fence down and Mama crossed over it, trying to get close enough to pitch the water on the cat, but it had another plan. The cat sprang to its feet and launched right for her. Mama jumped that fence and both she and Leslie literally ran for their lives back into the house! Linda's huge cat turned out to be a mountain lion.

It was not unusual for us to see wild animals around the house. Daddy had a fence around a garden to keep the deer from destroying it. You could hear birds of all kinds. Leslie learned to be a great imitator of their calls. We raised some animals too. We had chickens for both fresh eggs and to eat. Leslie was in charge of caring for them. He claimed that you could hypnotize a chicken by turning it upside down.

I could never figure out why someone would even want to hypnotize a chicken, but believed if anyone could he would be the one to know how. He spent hours upon hours with those chickens.

We kids we're so divided on our opinions of slaughtering day when Daddy would wring some of those chickens' necks. I was squeamish about the whole ordeal and took no part in it, except of course after Mama had them fried up and sitting on the dinner table.

Daddy tried to raise a couple of pigs once, but they were like family pets. Mama cried when the day came to butcher them, so they were sold instead. Blackberries grew wild along the creek bank and we kids would go pick them. The pricks we got from those thorny vines sure hurt, but one bite of Mama's blackberry cobbler covered in thick cream made it all worthwhile.

It is amazing that more kids never got hurt out in the boonies. Bobby was the only one who really suffered a tragedy out there. Daddy built a new fire every morning when it was needed. He dug a pit away from the house, where he dumped the coals from our pot belly stove. It took a long time for those old colds to burn out. Bobby always watched for us kids to come in from school and will run to meet us. On this one particular day, however, something else caught his eye. He saw the flicker of red coming from that pit and ran full force toward it. He fell in before we could catch him. By the time we could get to him, his little legs were terribly burned. Mama wrapped them up and rushed him to the emergency room. It was amazing that he ever learned to walk again, but the burns finally healed, and though he would never be a runner, Bobby does quite well walking now.

Even out there in the boonies, we always had Saturday night company. The grown-ups would play Canasta, and we kids would be in the living room listening to records and having dance contests. Verna was both the judge and a participant. The winner got a piece of Mama's fudge. Somehow, though few of us besides Verna won any of the contests, we all got more than our fair share of that sweet candy.

We were so excited when Aunt May and Uncle Cliff drove up from Los Angeles. Sometimes their oldest daughter and son-in-law, Dorothy and Art, would accompany them to visit us. We could hardly wait to see that shiny new Torino pull up into our driveway. Uncle Cliff always brought a movie camera and filmed us. He also had another fancy looking camera to take photographs. He would drive us kids up to the damn to swim. Mama would never let us go there alone. Uncle Cliff was a big sports fan and on

Sunday afternoon he drove to Lakeport, thirteen miles away, where we played in the city park while he watched the boat races. Aunt May, Mama's elder sister, was just a few years older than Uncle Cliff, though she never showed it. She was so pretty and gracious. Aunt May always liked for us girls to wash, comb and set her hair. We enjoyed doing that for her.

We had other visitors to from time to time. Nutty Nettie was one of those who would drop by once in a while. We kids did not know her real name. Of course, we did not call her nutty when she was around, except for once. Bobby and Glenn hid behind the couch where she was sitting, and then jumped up and down hollering "Nutty Nettie, Nutty Nettie." They were really good at embarrassing us like that.

Whenever we heard a car pull up to driveway and horn honk, that meant Hubert and his family were there. They seldom came inside back in those days, but we would go out and talk to them for hours in their car. He was such a funny guy. Mama had grown up with Hubert and his sister was her best friend.

Our house was always company-clean. We girls washed dishes from the time we could reach the sink by standing in a chair. Dirty dishes never sat at our house. They were done as soon as the meal was over. Usually, we did not mind doing dishes so much, but when there was company over, it seemed like we would never get finished. Our parents took great pride in their home. Almost every time we moved somewhere, the house we rented was a pigsty at first. But we would scrub down the walls and cabinets with Lysol, and Daddy laid new linoleum. He was an expert seamstress and kept our furniture and cars well upholstered. Our yard was always neat and clean too. We were poor, but we did our best with what revenue and talents the Lord gave us.

On Sunday mornings David Mills drove the church van out to our place to pick up kids. He was so good to drive all the way out to the boonies for us. We loved Sunday school and it was exciting to dress up once a week and go somewhere special.

Mrs. Mountain did not go to the same church as we did but she knew about us somehow. I believe she was a Seventh-day Adventist. She always came out during the summer to take us to Vacation Bible School where we learned many new songs and made crafts from plaster of

Paris and other things like little tiles or shells. That was always a great week of fun for us.

Right before Christmas, Mrs. Mountain would come again. We were especially happy to see her then because she would come with her car loaded down with huge Christmas stockings, gifts, and food. She made us feel special and we sort of thought of her as Mrs. Santa Claus.

Christmas was a fun time for us. The walnut season would end right before then, so Daddy saved a little money to buy us all something. We never got a whole lot of gifts but what we did get was cherished. A $2 locket was received like a prized possession.

I always felt bad, because so many times Mama and Daddy had not much of anything to open for themselves. They said their joy was in giving to us. Yes, Christmas must have been about the happiest day of the year for us and the only thing not good about it was that it fell just about the time the cold season began.

Chapter 9

Our Link To Civilization

We had to walk a mile to the creek and cross the bridge to catch the bus every day to school. That bridge was our only link to civilization. This was no ordinary bridge, believe me! It was an old, wooden bridge with boards missing here and there. Of the ones that were there, many were loose, would creak as we walked across them, and there were no side railings to hold on to for support. Most of the time we would cross that old rickety bridge relatively safely, but during the cold and dangerous season it was something else!

I knew with one slip; they would be pulling me out of the frigid creek below.

The other kids said that I had to cross it, or walk back home alone. It was too cold and dangerous to walk back that far by myself, so I did the only thing there was to do. Getting down on my hands and knees, I crawled across those icy boards with Verna on one side of me, and Leslie on the other. After they helped me, both of them had to go all the way back and literally pull Linda across. Both Linda and I were bawling our eyes out. We could see the bus was already at the stop, and wondered if Smitty would wait for us. We prayed never to have to go through that again.

Mama convinced Daddy that we would be safer living on the other side of Kelsey Creek, and that was answered prayer for me! The house we moved to was a lot smaller, but being a little cramped was worth never having to cross that old bridge again in the wintertime.

All six of us girls shared the loft bedroom. Verna got the small section to the left of the staircase, all to herself, because she was the oldest. Patty and I shared a bed, as did the three younger girls. Patty would wet the bed, and then roll me over, so she could sleep on my dry side. It took me a while to figure out why my side of the bed would be wet when my underwear was dry, but I finally caught on to what Patty was doing and put a stop to it. Linda had to sleep right in between Terri and Susie, because if she did not, the two little girls would kick each other. Poor Linda got peed on from both sides.

Leslie worked odd jobs for the landlord, and got paid mostly in goods rather than cash. Once in trade for his work she gave him a little travel trailer, and that was where he slept. The trailer seemed scary to me. He had knives and hatchets hanging all over the walls. But Leslie loved being out there in his own little place that he had earned for himself.

Mama sectioned off one part of the living room for a bedroom for the two little boys, and she and Daddy had a room downstairs too. For the most part they seemed happy there. Mama would whistle, snap her fingers, sing, and dance while she cooked and cleaned. Daddy would come in from work and tell us riddles or sing silly little short songs. Mama would get upset and throw things at Daddy and he would catch and calmly set them down, which made her even madder. She was a worrier and verbalized her fears a lot. Daddy was easy going for the most part, so they balanced each other out. The most important thing was we always knew they loved each other.

Daddy would pick Mama up and carry her around the house with her fussing at him to put her down. She would chase him from room to room with a deodorant can until he finally agreed to take a bath. We would be filled with excitement to see them romp around the house like that. It made us feel good to know that although they sometimes had spats; our parents did love each other.

Mama kept us as neat and clean as she did the house. Our hair was always brushed and fixed in braids or curled with a Toni permanent wave. The boys' hair was cut short and well-groomed. Our school clothes were always washed and pressed, and we knew to change into our play clothes as soon as we got home. Our school clothes were hung up once more before they were laundered.

Mama spent a lot of time with us girls and tried to teach us to be little ladies. She told us to walk balancing books on our heads, to stand straight up and take slow dainty steps. She kept us physically fit by using Debbie

Drake's exercise routines. She told us to hold in our tummies and if we looked a little plump, she would have us on a low-calorie diet for a while. Mama was proud of all of us, and everyone told her how beautiful we were.

Mama took care of herself too. I remember school parties that homeroom mothers would attend, and wished Mama could have come to some of those parties because she was far prettier than those other women. She looked like an angel to me with her fair skin, flowing golden hair, and blue eyes. She was quite talented as an amateur lyric writer and artist.

Mama drew angels and named them after us girls. We took them to school to show them off, and all of our friends would want one. They were the prettiest angels I'd ever seen, just like Mama.

It was quiet and peaceful out there around that canyon. So serene, in fact, that Glenn was swinging outside one day and rocked himself to sleep. He fell and broke his arm in two places.

In the springtime wildflowers sprung up everywhere. We would walk for miles along that country road gathering flowers as we went on our way. Mama had hay fever so we could not bring our bouquets into the house, but it was fun picking them anyway.

The spring rainy seasons we're all but calm. We girls watched the storms from the loft window. It seemed like the rain would never stop. The creek flooded over the back and was raging like a mighty river. We saw that old bridge crack into pieces and float away. The roots of the big tree between our place and the road gave way, and it came crashing down on the house. The tree fell through power lines. Hot wires danced all over the road, and we knew Daddy was going to be out there and were afraid he would be electrocuted.

We begged him not to go, but someone had to barricade the road to keep any traffic from driving into the dangerous and deadly mess. Thank God we all made it through that flood safely.

Aunt Bert and Uncle Babe lived next door and went through a similar flood with us. She was a happy lady who always had a story to tell. He was a funny guy who would sort of snicker when he laughed. Bert was not really our aunt, but Mama's cousin. Her parents died when she was young, and Grandpa Smith raised her as his own. Aunt Bert married Uncle Babe who had been divorced and had four kids in his ex-wife's custody. The two youngest were twin boys who started living with Aunt Bert and Uncle Babe when they were toddlers. We grew up thinking of them as our cousins. The twins Ray and Roy ("Hot Shot" and "Peewee") were good guitarist and we often had evening outdoor sing-alongs.

Sometimes Mama would leave us in Verna's charge. They bought potatoes by the hundred-pound bags and had no sooner backed the car out of the driveway when Verna would start peeling potatoes to be fried. She could get a little ornery when our folks weren't around.

Verna would make us all go outside and then lock the door and turn the record player up full blast. Patty got so mad at her for making faces at us through the front door window that she ran her fist right through that glass one time. Another time Verna was supposed to be fixing our lunch she brought in a sandwich and told Patty to close her eyes and take a bite. The sandwich was made from soap shavings!

Not long after that Verna, at age fifteen married Peewee. We had the reception at home. That was a fun time. We had all the chips and dips anyone could possibly eat and lots of sparkling punch. All our family and friends were there, and we played records and twisted all night to "Rock Around the Clock." The best thing about Verna getting married was Patty got her bed. I still had to share mine, but at least Linda did not wet the bed.

Leslie was another one who could be mischievous at times. He was the only boy in our family for so long and had been spoiled by both Grandma Renie and Daddy. Leslie hated sharing anything with us and never ever wanted us to follow him anywhere. I followed him once anyway, out to this roped footbridge that stretched across the canyon. Leslie was almost across when he looked back to see me near the middle, and then

he swung that bridge back and forth.
That sure broke me from tagging along
after him.

Once in a while Mama would tell
Leslie to stay home when she went to
Lakeport to grocery shop. I do not know
how he got there so fast, but Leslie
would hitchhike into town and be
standing there at the entrance of the
Safeway when Mama arrived.

Leslie also used to tell us to ask
Daddy to take him fishing. If we
refused, he would hit us. If Daddy would
be too busy to go fishing, Leslie would
hit us anyway. It was a no-win
situation.

He had been my hero throughout our younger days, but now that Leslie and I were both adolescents, we did not get along as well. Once during an exam, he kept whispering my name. I tried to ignore him. Then he started throwing spit wads at me. When I finally did look at him; Leslie motioned for me to go back to the pencil sharpener. He had not studied, and I knew he wanted the answers, but went back there anyway to keep him from disrupting the class any further. When I refused to give him the answers to the test, he grabbed me by the collar. The teacher saw him and scolded both of us out loud. That was so embarrassing, but at least it did make him leave me alone.

Kelsey Creek ran right in behind our place. We used to beg Mama to let us go swimming in early May. We could hardly wait to jump into the clear stream, but she always measured the water's temperature by the ending of the school year. During summer break, we stayed all day in the creek. All of us could swim from the time we were barely school-aged. We swam underwater as far as we could, downstream like little fish. We searched for interesting rocks on the creek bottom. By dinner time, we'd be dragging in waterlogged and sunbaked.

In order to get to the deepest swimming hole, we had to follow the path that ran alongside Mrs. Ryman's house. She'd always be working out in her yard in a sunbonnet and bathing suit. Once in a while she would come swimming too. Mrs. Rayman was sure comical looking with her round, wrinkled, little, old body in that bathing suit. She had a Shetland pony named Susie that was forever getting loose. We all helped her chase the pony back inside the fence.

Lake County was full of tourist in the summertime. This city family owned the cabin which sat on a little hill overlooking our place. They were there about two months out of every summer. One morning we would wake up to see their kids busy hoeing weeds.

When their work was done, the kids would head for the creek with a canoe and paddles. Sometimes they invited us to ride with them. Their oldest daughter would sit on the bank and sketch on drawing tablets.

Compared to us, they were rich. We could only imagine a lifestyle that afforded long summer vacations, a summer cabin, canoes, and drawing paper. We hated to see the family packing their station wagon back up again because that indicated summer would soon be over. Before you know it, we kids would be standing across the road listening for the honk of our school bus echoing through the canyon.

You could not beat Smitty for a bus driver. He got along well with all the kids on our route. In the winter he sometimes even would open the door and let us put every window down and play freeze out. It seemed like it took us forever to get home from school though. We were near the end of the route. Once we reached the canyon, time flew by because Smitty would take those curves pretty fast and honk as we rounded blind corners. We were tossed to and fro on the seat, and sometimes even fell into the aisles, but we enjoyed that canyon roller coaster ride, laughing all the way through it!

One day when the bus came to a stop in front of our house the laughter subsided. My heart sank. The sideboards were on the pickup, and I knew we would be gone again before nightfall.

Chapter 10

A Town Called Finley

The little house next to our church was vacant and the church offered to rent it to Daddy for $50 a month. It was hard to leave behind all those memories we had made in the boonies, but it was sort of exciting to actually be moving into town again. You can walk from one end of Finley to the other side in five minutes tops. In those days all it had was a service station, Chinese restaurant and bar, convenience store, and church.

No Church would ever begin to compare to the memories I had in Big Valley

Community Church there in Finley. The words of those old cherished hymns will forever ring in my heart. We loved to hear the special music done with the accordion accompaniment. Sometimes the girls would have special music too. The twins Hot Shot and Pee Wee, and Verna and Patty wrote a touching song that they sang for the church.

Members of the church were so good to our family and made us feel welcome. We never felt poor or out of place there. Our teachers were kind and told us interesting Bible stories, using colorful felt-board characters and scenery. We always had a memory verse to learn and recite. At Easter and Christmas, we had plays to perform and it was fun getting dressed in biblical costumes, setting up props, and acting out our parts. We also went out in caroling groups, which warmed hearts with an old-fashioned Christmas spirit.

We had a penny march at church that was a lot of fun for us kids, especially when we were really young. The first time Leslie ever participated in it he thought the money was given to him and stuffed his pockets full of coins.

We attended socials at the church too once in a while. There was an annual picnic we always had either at Highland

Springs Dam or Lake Port City Park. I always wanted to be baptized then but Mama felt that I was not old enough to understand its full meaning and would not give her permission.

Occasionally, the church would take us skating at the nearest rink in Ukiah, about forty miles away. We did not know how to skate, but the adults would either carry us or hold us up so that we did not fall. Our pastor was a short, jolly, little, Swedish man, who sometimes had problems with English. I loved to hear him speak. Right in the middle of his sermon it'd be all quiet and still, and suddenly an older lady would stand up and give a message in tongues, which she interpreted for us. It took us kids by surprise every time and we nearly jumped out of our seats!

I found salvation in that little church. Patty and I both responded to the same altar call. Such a holy presence was there that it felt as though we could have reached out and touched the hand of God.

The only bad thing about living in the church's little house was that the bar was across the road from us. There were cars constantly pulling in and out of the parking lot, and it took us a while to adjust to the noise of city life. Someone stole our car right out of our driveway. The police found it some hours later. Someone had run it off Hopland Mountain.

That summer Patty and Leslie got to ride the bus to Los Angeles to visit Aunt May and Uncle Cliff for a few weeks. Verna had gone the year before, and I could not wait for my turn next year. One got to do all kinds of things there that we kids only dreamed about, like going to Disneyland and Knott's Berry Farm. We also received a weekly allowance. The only money I ever had of my own was when someone paid me for babysitting once in a blue moon.

Aunt Marie, Daddy's oldest sister, lived in Finley too for a while. She and Uncle Roscoe had three sons, and the younger two used to play house with us. It was so much fun having boys to play the role of daddy. Mama would give us old mail-order catalogs and we'd cut the models out to use as paper dolls. We made most of our own toys.

Sometimes we'd step on tin cans and walk with them stuck to our shoes, pretending they were high heels. We'd tie two cans to the opposite ends of a piece of twine and use it for a telephone. We would hold to the cloth belts of our dresses and pretend to be holding the reins of a horse. Sometimes you would find us astride an old broom handle that we called our horse when we played "Cowboys and Indians" for hours shooting at each other with stick guns or make-believe arrows. We played "War" and imitated the sound of machine guns too. We had jousting bouts with cane swords. We made families out of oak balls using sticks for their extremities.

When the weather was too bad outside, we had games to play indoors such as hide-n-seek, Button-Button, Doctor-Doctor, Rotten Egg, and Spend the Bottle. Mama had a big canister full of buttons and we would sort through them for hours. They were like shiny gems to us.

Once in a while Shirley would come. She had lived next door to us years ago in Burnett's Cabins. Shirley was my best friend, Judy's mother. She was a real sweet lady and talked so loudly and fast it was hard for me to understand her. I got a kick out of listening to her. Judy and I took long walks around town while Mama and Shirley drank coffee and visited.

Occasionally I got to spend the night with Judy. Those mornings, Shirley would get us up and have toast and coffee ready. What a strange thing for me! Mama always fixed us hot cereal. It was great getting to drink coffee. Shirley put lots of milk in it, but still I was having coffee just like a grown up.

It was so nice to be best friends with the daughter of Mama's best friend. It was like the cycle of history repeating itself through our generation. Life was good in that little town called Finley.

Chapter 11

The Intruder

When we moved from Finley Mama and Daddy rented a place from the Wild's family, that was spacious and nice enough, but the problem was with the location. It sat between Kelseyville and Lakeport. We were in Lakeport School District. The Indians and the Cardinals were longtime rivals and there was no way I wanted to go to Lakeport School. I felt like a traitor.

Lakeport is the county seat and a bigger town, so their school system had a little different setup, fifth through eighth grade went to Terrace School. I was in the seventh grade and in Kelseyville would have still attended the elementary school.

It was sort of neat to go to Junior High. The teachers were nice, and I was able to make new friends fairly easily, so going to Lakeport School turned out not to be so bad after all.

I was eleven years old then and really felt big. Mama and Daddy both smoked, and it seemed like the grown-up thing to do so I would sneak into their cigarettes and smoke them at the dried-up creek bed near our place. The little kids caught me once, though, and told Mama, so my smoking days were over. I was not the only one of us kids who were ever caught trying to light up a time or two. Patty and her best friend were out with our cousin and another boy and ended up in a car wreck, which broke Patty's collarbone. Daddy removed the mattress from her bed to put a sheet of wood under it because Patty needed to sleep on a hard surface while the break healed. What did he find: a pack of cigarettes stashed between the mattress and box springs. Of course, she swore that they were not hers, but we all knew better.

Patty got married soon after that. Like Verna, she was only fifteen. Patty married Hot Shot, just a year after Verna and Pee Wee's wedding. Linda and I dressed alike this time— Mama's idea not ours. The good thing about Patty getting married was now I was the oldest girl at home. The bad part was there was less help with those chores.

Daddy raised a big garden there at the Wild's place. It seemed one day he would be standing there with the corn barely breaking through the soil and before we knew it those stalks would be shoulder high. There's nothing like the taste of a fresh ear of corn smothered in butter that drips down your chin when you take a bite. Daddy's teeth were in bad shape and Mama would cut the corn off the cob so he could eat it. He never went to the dentist back in those days. When a tooth would give him trouble, he would pull it out with pliers and end the agony for a while! He never complained but I sure felt sorry for him.

Despite the dental problems, Daddy would eat almost anything. For a small man he had a big appetite and Mama always had dinner ready when he got home from work. Daddy was the first to the table and the last to leave. Since we seldom had dessert, he would make his own by dipping pieces of bread into mixture of commodity corn syrup and butter.

During Walnut season that year while Daddy was working nights at the dehydrator, I saw the headlights of the car as it pulled into our driveway. I ran to unlock the door for Daddy, and then hurried back to bed. The room in which Linda and I slept did not have a door, so mama had hung a curtain up for our privacy.

I heard Daddy come in the front door and walk through the hall. He stopped outside of our room, pulled open the curtain, and briefly peeked inside. That seemed strange to me because Daddy never checked in on us girls like that before. He only stopped in our room for a brief moment, and then went on down the hall to his and Mama's room.

Before I knew it, he walked back outside got in the car and drove off. Mama jumped up, ran to lock the door, then back into our room screaming, "Who let that man in here!"

It was not Daddy! I had unlocked the door for a total stranger. Mama said that he must have been drunk or something and thought he was at his own home. When he got to her room, the man stood there looking totally confused. She had caught a glimpse of his reflection in the mirror and immediately knew it was not Daddy. She was paralyzed from fear and could not move a muscle so pretended she was asleep. Evidently, the man did not intend to harm any of us. From then on, I made sure who it was before letting anyone into our home.

We did not live at the Wild's place for very long, but I did finish out seventh grade there. I was looking forward to attending eighth grade because it was a big steppingstone into High School. I could not believe my ears when Mama told me we were moving to Oklahoma again. Moving!

I hated that word. No one ever asked what I felt was important enough to take with us. There was not room enough to take much of anything, so many memories were classified as an essential and would be left behind. There was no way I could ever get ready to leave all of our friends, the school, the church, but ready or not we were loaded up and Oklahoma bound.

So here I am in Broken Arrow standing out in the cold watching the firemen hopelessly trying to battle the blaze that was destroying our every possession. Here I am feeling so confused about the whole ordeal. Here I am hoping to finally get to go back home

again.

Chapter 12

Home Before High School

Dear Daddy, it's me Sandy. The Lord only knows how many times I've attempted to tell you this but just couldn't find the courage to do so. I was afraid you would not understand. How could you when I cannot even comprehend it myself? Here lately though things have been clearer, and I am understanding myself much better, which has helped me come to the point of being able to write you this letter.

Daddy, for as long as I can remember we spent our lives moving from one house to another, from California to Arizona to Oklahoma and then back to California again. There are twenty different places that I could name where we lived. It was a terrible thing many times to get off the school bus knowing I would not be getting back on it the next morning. We could not even say goodbye to our friends, teachers, or church members. We would just be there today and gone tomorrow.

By sunset you would have the trailer pickup loaded up, and we would be piled into the car like a bunch of sardines. We were all so cranky from being overcrowded. Mama was uncomfortable. Remember how she sat on those loaves of bread to ease the soreness in her behind? You would drive until you could not keep your eyes open any longer and then pull off the highway to rest a little while.

By then we kids had been lulled to sleep by the engines hum and when the car stopped, we'd all wake up. We were tired and irritable and fussed back and forth, forcing you outside to try and find a little peace and quiet. You would lay across the hood of the car. It could not have been a very restful nap because you were never out there for long.

You would pull over to fill the gas tank and we would all tumble out and make a mad dash for the restrooms. It would be a long wait before our next bathroom stop. We older ones would help the little kids out "Terri cloth", "Bobby Pin", and "Glenny Pig", but little independent "Susie Q" would just snap, "No! I can get out by myself."

She and the other little munchkins already had the car smelling like an ammonia factory, not to mention the scent of car sickness with which Patty always blessed us. I bet we were a sight—nine kids, of all ages and sizes, with our hair sticking straight up in the air. Our clothes were wrinkled. Barefoot, holding each other's hands and running for the toilet, we hollered at one to hurry up so the next one could use the restroom.

Though the travel was tiresome, it was not always boring. We were fascinated by the desert jumping cacti and tumbleweeds. There were Indian teepees and Navajo Villages set up in the hillsides. There were interesting totem poles near Indio California. We traveled past the Painted Desert, plateaus, and huge boulders throughout Mexico somehow balanced atop one another. We saw U.S. cities lit up at night with dazzling brilliance and long country miles with nothing to see but an occasional farmhouse and a cow or two. We crossed flatlands, rolling plains, and of course mountains. No one who had ever crossed the Tehachapi Mountain before its major road repairs could ever forget that dangerous pass.

El Mirage would either be the getting off place or the halfway mark, where we'd get a bath hot meal and a good night sleep at Grandma's house. The car would be cleaned out too so we could head out the next day or two a lot more comfortable and refreshed. Our journey would reach its end in Oklahoma, another 24 hours of near-constant travel.

You would, after much searching, finally convince some landlord that eleven people could live in a three-bedroom house without destroying the place. We would unload and set up housekeeping. You always found work somewhere, and although sometimes dinner meant a pot of noodles or beans, we never went hungry.

The new had hardly worn off of our house, school, and friendships before we were loaded back up and headed home again. Of course, leaving Oklahoma or Arizona was never quite as bad as leaving California because what few roots we had were all in Lake County, but still we had made new friends and grown attached to some of our teachers. It was leaving these people behind probably never to see them again that really hurt.

As I grew older, I began to build barriers to protect myself from getting hurt any further. It was easier to not make friends than it was to have to leave them. It was easier to feel lonely than to try to be accepted into some established click, where I just did not fit in. It was easier to hate school than to care about trying to catch up in some strange curriculum.

So, I started playing hooky and sometimes Mama kept me home to watch the boys while she ran errands. Babysitting was so much easier for me than going to school.

I was in eighth grade when we moved to Broken Arrow. As with all other places, we kids enrolled ourselves in school. I was not happy there at all. There was one girl, who lived down the road from us, and we sort of became friends, but she was not in any of my classes. Once we got off the bus in the morning, we did not see each other again until after school was out.

I missed my friends back home so badly and thought of running away many times. That house we had in Broken Arrow was probably the nicest place we ever had, but I did not want to stay in Oklahoma. Staying there meant I'd never go home, and I just had to get back home. We did not belong in Oklahoma! We did not even speak the language! Our accents revealed that California was our own. I absolutely had to do something to correct this wrong. I had to do something to get us back where we belonged.

It was chilly that one morning that Mama and Aunt Bonnie had gone shopping and left the boys with me. Today was the day I told myself. I began to plan my escape. With a sack full of sandwiches and the boys all bundled up, we set out walking. It was so cold the boys were freezing. With each step we took, reality kept haunting me. What was I thinking? We had to turn around and go back to the house before we all froze to death. Still my mind kept searching for ways to get back to California.

All of my friends there would be graduated from grade school in a few months and going on that traditional eighth grade trip to the planetarium in Sacramento and San Francisco's

Chinatown. So, they would be starting High School. I wanted, needed to go to high school with my friends back home.

That morning I was heating water to wash the breakfast dishes and we had no water heater in that home. Any warm water had to be boiled in a big pot on top of the stove. The burners' flame seemed to be hypnotizing me, providing me through my trance with an idea. But would it work? Sure, it would! And I was desperate enough to make it happen.

I chased the boys outside near the road and ordered them to stay put, and then ran back inside and found a couple of cans of lighter fluid Mama kept in the cabinet. I used up the half empty can first on all the furniture and then squirted the other can on the floors, walls, and ceilings all throughout the house. I went into your room and lit a couple of matches. Then I shut the door and checked on the boys. For once they were obedient and kept playing in the yard.

I ran back to check on the fires progression. Your closet was already burned. I grabbed some of Mama's favorite clothing and threw them out under the tree. I wanted to go back in and save a few more things, but by then fire had spread everywhere so I hurried over to the boys and held them tightly. My heart was pounding! My mind was racing! I was crying so hard, harder than ever before. I had never been so scared in my entire life.

Before I knew it, there were firemen everywhere and Uncle Jerry was there talking with them. They told me not to cry and said it was not my fault. They called me a hero for saving the boys and said everything would be all right. But I was no hero and it was my entire fault. If they only knew.

We did not go back home right away. Instead we lived in a little cabin near Uncle Jerry and Aunt Bonnie's house for a while. There we had to draw water from a well. It was not nice like the other place, and we were super cramped in that little shack.

The story of our fire hit the local newspaper. It was big time news for that small town and the whole town came to our rescue. Church groups brought us furniture, food, clothing, and housekeeping necessities. Local merchants had us come to their stores to pick out things such as shoes and toothbrushes. We had better things now than what had burnt. All of the townspeople were so good to us. I wondered if you and Mama would choose to stay in Broken Arrow, but you did not. However, you didn't go home right then either.

Patty and Hot Shot had also moved to Broken Arrow and I stayed with them while you moved the rest of the family to Tishomingo. By summer you came back for me, and finally we were going home. For the intended purpose of comfort, Leslie, Linda and I were sent ahead with Patty and Hot Shot a couple of days before you. What a trip that was!

I'll never forget it and I thought all those other trips we had made were bad, but this one was ridiculous! The car kept breaking down and it took most all of our grocery money to get it fixed. We were lucky to get a donut in the morning and a hotdog for lunch. We certainly were not comfortable as there was no room to even try to lay down. We had to sleep sitting up.

The only good thing about this trip was there were no little ones to stink up the car. That old junk heap of a car died near Stockton, never to budge again. Buster came to pick us up. He drove far too fast over St. Helena Mountain, making unsafe passes around dangerous blind curves. I felt like we were on one huge roller coaster ride, and prayed to God we would even live to see home again. I was never so relieved in my life than when we pulled up into Grandma Burnett's driveway.

She rented a cabin to Patty and Hot Shot, where we stayed for a couple of days before you and the rest of the family got into town. I do not remember what or if we had anything to eat over those couple of days. By then, I was in a daze because everything that had transpired was pressing hard on my heart and mind.

We moved back to that little house around Kelsey Creek Canyon. I got to babysit that summer and earn enough money to buy some nice school clothes.

I remember how hard it was to wait across the road that first day school was back in session. I anxiously awaited the familiar songs of Smitty's horn echoing through the canyon. It felt so right to board his bus. Finally, thank God, I was home before high school.

But nothing went as I hoped it would. I was so looking forward to that reunion with my old friends, but something happened while we were away. My friends changed, or maybe I had, but there was a definite difference. The kids I had played with when we were shorter than the hollyhocks, now barely acknowledged me. They were all wrapped up in other people and things. I was lucky to get a passing hello from any of them. This just could not be happening to me! It was like a living nightmare. I was treated like a new kid in my own School.

That is when the awful truth hit me. Everything I had done was in vain. It took my burning down our home to get back to where I fit in, only to discover that I no longer felt welcomed. I felt that this must be my punishment. Guilt began to set in. I carried that guilt around for the past 23 years.

Finally, I am able to lay all that pain at the foot of the cross. Finally, I'm able to tell you I am sorry for the pain I caused you and the family. It must have been terrible for you to be called home from work to such an awful sight. All of your hard work must have seemed so pointless at the time because everything we owned, all you had provided for us, every photograph, and every document was turned to ashes.

Daddy, I want you to know that it was hard for me too. I wish so many times that there had been some other way out for me. Believe me, the burden of guilt I bore for so long was no easy load to haul. Well, it is not my secret anymore. I feel better for having told you what really happened that day, and by telling you, I have been able to come to terms with it myself and tell the rest of our family.

It is only in having grown a little older and a lot more mature that I finally realized what those firemen said to me was partially correct.

It really was not all my fault.

I love you, Daddy, always.

Sandy

Made in the USA
Middletown, DE
23 September 2023

38929899R00090